First Questions and Answers about the Earth

Are There Diamonds in My Backyard?

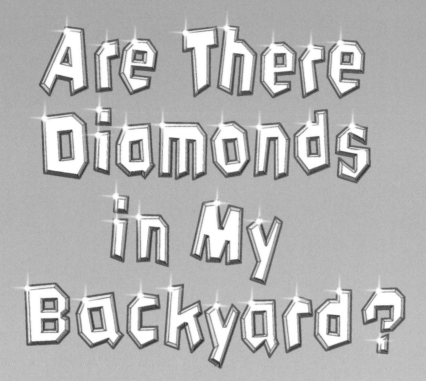

TIME
LIFE for
Children ®

ALEXANDRIA, VIRGINIA

Contents

Why are there so many rocks?   4

Why are rocks hard?   6

Why are rocks so many different shapes and colors?   8

Are there diamonds in my backyard?   10

Can I dig all the way to China?   12

Where does water come from?   14

What made this cave?   16

What are those big machines doing?   18

What else is under the ground?   20

What makes mountains?   22

How tall is the world's tallest mountain?   24

How did this lake get up here?   26

What made the Grand Canyon?   28

Why are the canyon walls striped?   30

What happens in an earthquake?   32

What is a geyser?   34

Why do volcanoes erupt?   36

How many volcanoes are there?   38

Can I stand on the edge of the earth?   40

What is an island?   42

Why is earth called the blue planet?   44

Why is earth so special?   46

Why are there so many rocks?

Because the earth is a giant ball of rock! All the rocks and boulders we see were once part of thick layers of rock under the ground. Over many years, hot sun and freezing cold broke up some of the underground rock into the rocks, pebbles, sand, and mud that are all around us today.

5

Why are rocks hard?

Rocks are hard because they are made of minerals. Minerals are the tiny, hard specks you see when you look at a rock up-close.

The way rocks form inside the earth also makes them hard.

Granite

Obsidian

Basalt

I'm not a rock! I don't move that slowly!

Some rocks are made by fiery heat that melts minerals together. When the minerals cool, they turn into hard rock.

Sandstone

Shale

Limestone

Other rocks are made when
bits of broken rock and shell
pile up and press together.

Still other rocks form when old
rock is heated and squeezed.
Shale becomes slate and
limestone changes
to marble.

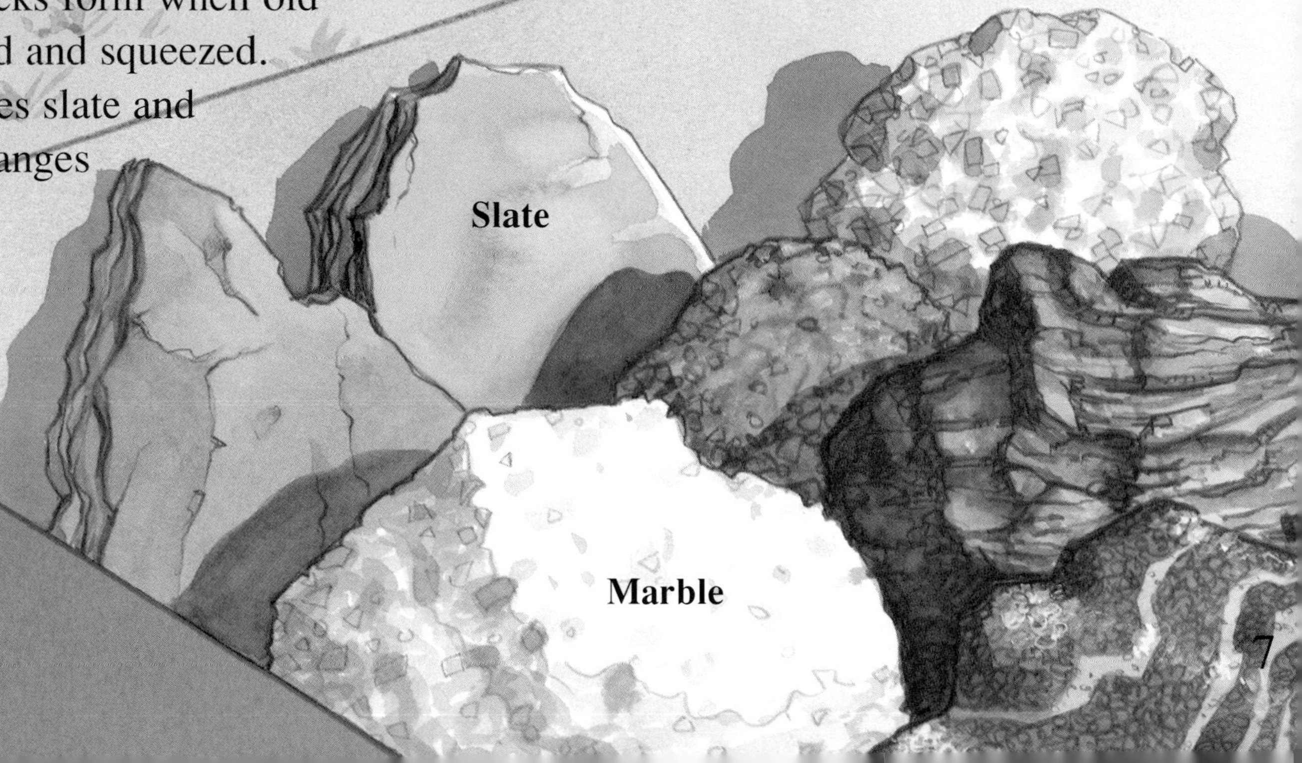

Slate

Marble

Why are rocks so many different shapes and colors?

Because rocks are made of minerals that have so many shapes and colors. Minerals combine to form different kinds of rocks—just as different toy blocks can stack into a variey of towers.

Rocks are also shaped by wind and water. Waves tumble pebbles until they are round and smooth. Sand blown by wind carves holes in boulders and cliffs.

Try it!

How many different rocks can you find? Put the small ones in an empty egg carton and the big ones in a shoebox. Now you're a rock hound!

Are there diamonds in my backyard?

Probably not. But even if there were, you would have a tough time finding them. Diamonds look like lots of other rocks and minerals when we find them in the ground. Only when they are cut and polished with special tools do they turn into sparkly jewels.

But you might find other beautiful minerals like these:

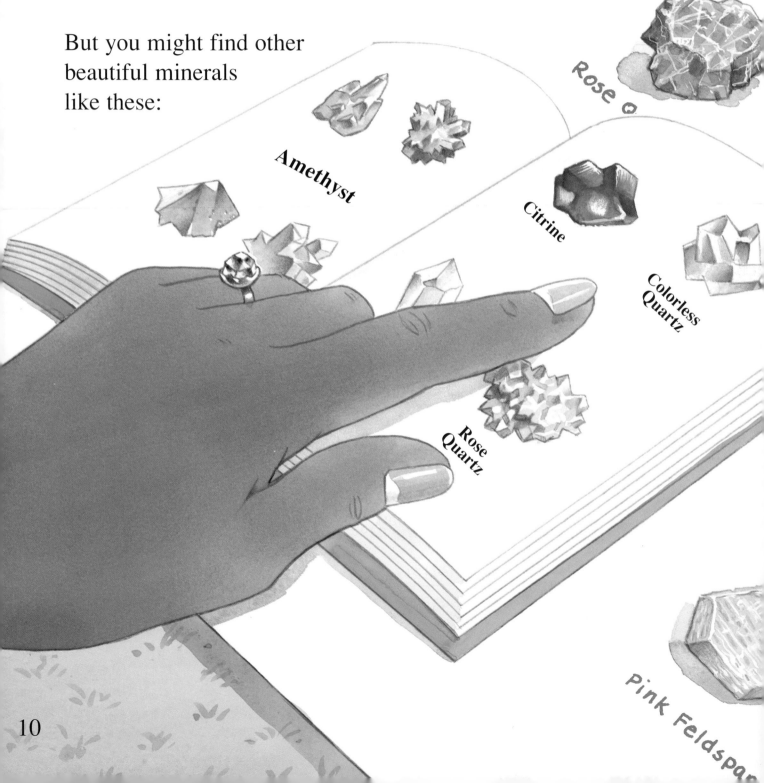

Rose Q

Amethyst

Citrine

Colorless Quartz

Rose Quartz

Pink Feldspar

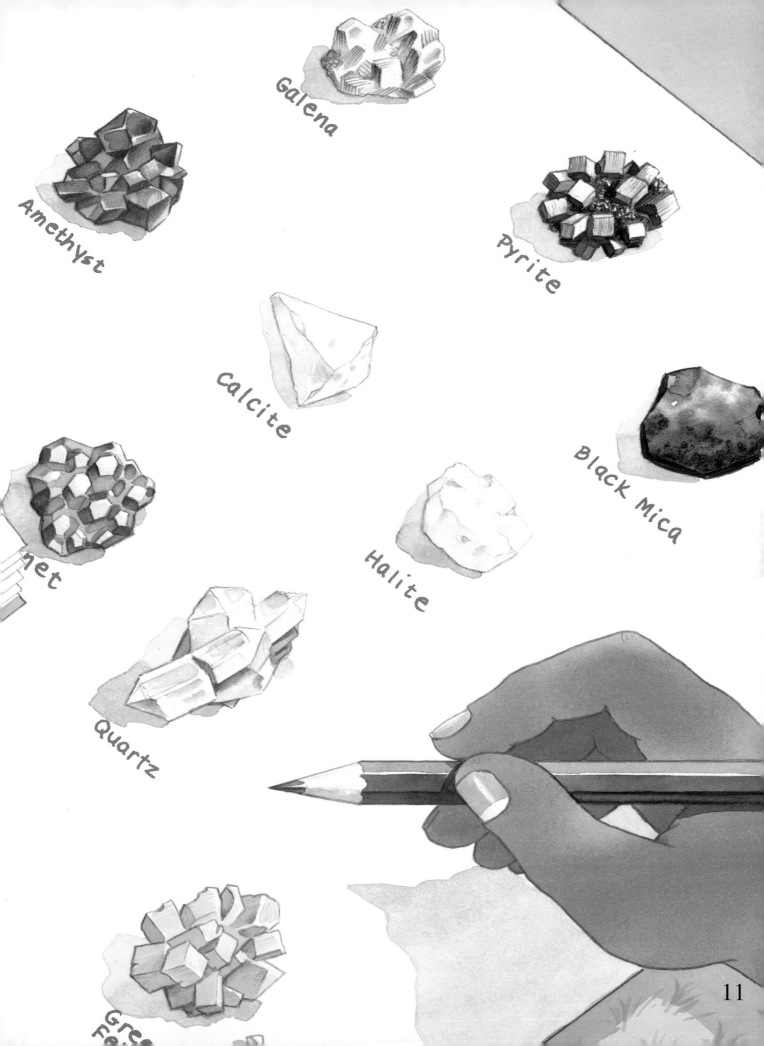

Galena

Amethyst

Pyrite

Calcite

Black Mica

net

Halite

Quartz

Gre
Fe

11

Can I dig all the way to China?

No one—not even with the help of the best digging machines—can dig all the way through the earth to China. There's just too much rock in the way!

Under the dirt in your yard are thick layers of solid rock. Underneath that rock is a deep layer of hot melted rock. And under *that* is more solid rock. If you want to go to China, you'll have to go around the earth, not through it!

Did you know?
The earth's top layer of rock is called the crust.

What made this cave?

Running, flowing, dripping water made it. When water seeps into the ground, it can slowly wear down the rock underneath. Some types of rock like limestone are easily worn away. When water rushes over limestone for a long time, it makes holes in the rock. The holes become the rooms and tunnels of a cave.

Stalagmites grow from the ground up!

Stalactites grow from the ceiling down!

Did you know?
Never explore a cave or opening in the ground without an adult!

What are those big machines doing?

Those machines are pumps. They are pulling up a liquid called oil that is buried deep in the earth. First, powerful drills cut through underground rock to make a passageway for the oil. Then the pumps bring it up. Oil is used to make the fuel that powers our cars, heats our homes, and runs all kinds of machines.

Did you know?

Plastic is made from a type of oil called petroleum. Your bright plastic toys started out as black oil deep underground!

What else is under the ground?

All sorts of minerals are dug up and made into metal objects that we use every day.

Steel for cars and airplanes comes from iron ore.

Aluminum ore is used for cans, pots, pans, and aluminum foil.

Precious metals like gold and silver are made into jewelry.

Copper is used to make pipes.

What makes mountains?

Mountains are made when the earth's crust moves. Some mountains form when parts of the crust squeeze together. The squeezing makes the crust fold and wrinkle into a mountain. Other mountains form when the crust breaks. One piece of crust pushes up higher than the other. When this happens, mountains are built.

The earth's crust moves very, very slowly. It takes millions of years to build a mountain.

Did you know?

Some mountains are very young and some are very old. Young mountains are tall with jagged, snow-covered tops. Older mountains are low with smooth, round tops.

23

How tall is the world's tallest mountain?

Any mountain seems tall when you're climbing it. But most mountains aren't even half as high as the world's tallest mountain. It's called Mount Everest. It is 29,078 feet tall, as tall as you would be if you stood on thousands of your friends' shoulders!

FAMOUS MOUNTAINS

Mt. Everest, Asia
29,078 feet

Mt. Aconcagua, South America
22,835 feet

Mt. McKinley, North America
20,321 feet

Mt. Kilimanjaro, Africa
19,341 feet

Mt. El'brus, Europe
18,510 feet

Did you know?

Big fields of ice on high mountains are called glaciers. As glaciers move and melt, they slowly carve and reshape the mountainside.

How did this lake get up here?

Millions of years ago an icy glacier carved out a big bowl in the mountainside. When the glacier melted, the bowl filled with water to become a lake. Rainwater and melted snow keep the lake full of fresh water. How would you like to swim in a cold mountain lake?

Me next!

Did you know?

Lakes are smaller than oceans. They usually have fresh water while ocean water is salty.

What made the Grand Canyon?

Water—powerful, rushing water. Millions of years ago, the
Colorado River began to flow over the earth's rocky surface.
Over time river water cut a path in the rock. The water carried
stones and mud that helped cut even deeper. The path is now
the Grand Canyon.

Did you know?

The Colorado River is still carving out rock. Every hundred years, the Grand Canyon gets about one-half inch deeper.

Why are the canyon walls striped?

The colored stripes are layers of rock. Over many years, gravel, shells, sand, and mud settled in layers to form different kinds of rocks. New rock continues to form on top of old rock underneath.

Those layers of rock are almost two billion years old!

Try it!

Spread a layer of dirt in the bottom of a jar. Put a layer of sand on top, then a layer of pebbles. Look through the sides to see the stripes.

What happens in an earthquake?

The ground shakes! In most places the earth's crust moves so slowly you can't feel it. But in certain places, there are cracks in the earth's crust. The cracks are called faults. When the earth moves at a fault, the crust on one side bumps and slides against the crust on the other. That makes the ground tremble and shake.

Aahhhhhh!

Did you know?
Buildings near faults are often specially built for safety in an earthquake.

33

What is a geyser?

It's an opening in the ground where big fountains of water and steam spray up into the air. Under the geyser is a pool of water heated by hot rocks. Some of the water turns into steam. When the steam and hot water push against the rocky layers above, they burst out in a giant spout called a geyser.

Did you know?

A geyser in Yellowstone National Park acts like it has a clock inside it. It erupts almost every hour of the day and night. That's why it is called Old Faithful.

Why do volcanoes erupt?

Volcanoes erupt when hot melted rock deep underground pushes up and bursts out through a crack in the earth's crust. The melted rock is called lava. When the lava cools down, it turns into hard rock. As the hardened lava piles up, the volcano grows into a steep-sided mountain.

How many volcanoes are there?

There are about 500 volcanoes that still spout lava. Most of them are found around the Pacific Ocean. These volcanoes are carefully watched by scientists. They warn people nearby when they believe an eruption is going to take place.

Did you know?

The islands of Hawaii and Japan—located in the Pacific Ocean—were formed by volcanoes.

Can I stand on the edge of the earth?

No, because the earth has no edge. It's round like a ball. From the beach, the ocean looks like a flat stretch of water with a faraway edge. But in fact, the earth curves at this edge, called the horizon. If you could sail across the water, you would not fall off. Instead you would reach more land.

Did you know?

The earth's ocean is divided by seven huge pieces of land. They are called continents.

What is an island?

An island is a piece of land that has water all around it. Some islands are chunks of continents that were separated from the mainland by rising water. Others are the tops of old volcanoes that don't erupt anymore. Still others are made of the hard skeletons of tiny sea animals called coral.

43

Why is earth called the blue planet?

Because a huge blue ocean covers most of it. In pictures taken from space, the earth looks like a bright blue ball. So people call it the blue planet. The earth's water makes it the only known planet where plants and animals can live and grow.

Why is the earth so special?

The earth gives us almost everything we need to live healthy lives: food to eat, water to drink, fuel to heat our homes, and minerals to make the many things we use every day. Its mountains, lakes, streams, and oceans are beautiful places for us to visit and enjoy. It's hard to imagine living in a better world!

TIME-LIFE for CHILDREN®

Managing Editor: Patricia Daniels
Editorial Directors: Jean Burke Crawford,
    Allan Fallow, Sara Mark
Senior Art Director: Susan K. White
Publishing Associate: Marike van der Veen
Administrative Assistant: Mary M. Saxton
Production Manager: Marlene Zack
Senior Copyeditor: Colette Stockum
Quality Assurance Manager: Miriam P. Newton
Library: Louise D. Forstall, Anne Heising

Special Contributor: Barbara Klein, Mary Anna Coons
Researcher: Jocelyn Lindsay
Writer: Jacqueline A. Ball

Designed by: David Bennett Books

Series design: David Bennett
Book design: David Bennett
Art direction: David Bennett
Design Administration: Sarah York
Illustrated by: Michael Brownlow
**Additional cover
 illustrations by:** Nick Baxter

First printing. Printed in U.S.A.
Published simultaneously in Canada.

Time Life Inc. is a wholly owned subsidiary of THE TIME INC. BOOK COMPANY.

TIME-LIFE is a trademark of Time Warner Inc. U.S.A.
For subscription information, call 1-800-621-7026.

Library of Congress Cataloging-in-Publication Data

Are there diamonds in my backyard? : first questions and answers about the earth.
    p. cm.—(Time-Life Library of first questions and answers)
        ISBN 0-7835-0902-2 (hardcover)
1. Earth sciences—Miscellanea—Juvenile literature. I. Time-Life for Children (Firm)
    II. Series: Library of first questions and answers.
QE 29.A68 1995   95-12423
550—dc20   CIP
                                                              AC

Consultants

Dr. Lewis P. Lipsitt, an internationally recognized specialist on childhood development, was the 1990 recipient of the Nicholas Hobbs Award for science in the service of children. He has served as the science director for the American Psychological Association and is a professor of psychology and medical science at Brown University.

Dr. Judith A. Schickendanz, an authority on the education of preschool children, is an associate professor of early childhood education at the Boston University School of Education, where she also directs the Early Childhood Learning Laboratory. Her published work includes *More Than the ABCs: Early Stages of Reading and Writing* as well as several textbooks and many scholarly papers.

Dr. George C. Stephens, chairman of the geology department at The George Washington University in Washington D.C., specializes in mountain-building processes and the evolution of glacial landscapes. Currently Dr. Stephens is studying the geologic evolution of the Andes Mountains.